BOMBLAST OR BREAKFAST?

POEMS

BOMBLAST OR BREAKFAST?

POEMS

by

J. Obii J. Nwachukwu-Agbada

AFRICAN HERITAGE PRESS

NEW YORK   LAGOS   LONDON

2017

INTROIT

ODE TO WAR

To those who smitten by fun spoil for war
Who triumph only when others swoon
They who plot their plunder in wound
I offer this slice of ode doled to war

Through years of guilt numbering scores
Out of the sins of unimpeded scofflaws
Come the grip of the renegades' claws
See them toy with humanity's jaws

See the puppet president's scraggy scroll
Spread on the wall to read a weary war
Even as he holds in his helpless hands
A fled shot aimed at unbothered hounds

Swan songs of war, sedate, claim the lull
Pained, we reminisce on the missed ball
And in the war room bald-headed bores
Prance like ahoy-men in drawling brawls

From the impassioned pomp at the seashore
Crew men snore & snort like drunken rams
And cavort & carouse on the slim seesaw
Where they flex their menopaused arms

Upon hearing the anthem of war blast
Saints sad, solemn appear by their tombs
Fortune hunters leap over their breakfast,
And do a beeline for weird martial tunes

At the sight of blown bombs in war
Inconsolable mums strop & scream
And war itself like a wanton whore
Dozes as in a dissonant dream

See the Bosses, fitful at their vast feat
As they daily stoke passions into war
While paper doll countries in defeat
Retreat, trembling in penitent awe

Look at the jamb of the wooden door
Reclined on it are those hawking war
Outside, the King's dog worried, gawks
The king of dogs gapes at the war hawks

NOT AN OWEN THOUGH

I once heard it whispered mouth to ear
that to locate the worthy word,
the famed phrase
to be certified a true poet of war
Owen, the Welsh who loved
the feeling word, the tearful term
went in quest of the word in war
And met one in one world war
In crutches, his face furrowed in pain
hemmed in on both sides
he rested his frame on a bed in a war hospice
from whence he scripted those tearful lines
about the mowing down of men
on the Somme, the mountain range of France
where the clay, having grown tall, was torched
But Owen lay on a hollow bed
in a hollow war-chest on rest
at Craiglockhart in the heart of Edinburg
Thus our poet lived & died
for war as a war pet, as a war poet

For sure, I'm not an Owen though
I mean the man who knew
how to mine the mind for mourning
the wizard of furrowed words in pain
in worried lines
in morbid stanzas of sorrow
I seek to gather neither pip nor point
nor point at anything beyond my occiput
War is not a craft, but poetry is.

RUMORS OF WAR

I hear another war is being brewed
boiling in the bath waters of war lords
another war is fawning to be fought
Let me leave as the wily one has left
his house of shell on his shoulders
Except the noise of an odious fart
the tortoise is usually not amused
when he hears the shout of a shell
Ask *alii!*

Listen: I haven't been to war before,
nor have I seen a raw war rage
nor seen a trenchant war in a war trench
Here, I paint my kind as victuals of war
the woes and clichés of war
the worms weaned by war
It is my doleful diploma which demands
I query the war lords and witches
who daily boast with bones
                              and crossbones
who ululate, seated atop the game
                              caught in war

Having left smoked fish to fish-mongers
shall we also leave war to war-mongers?
Brothers, rumors of war torture like war!
How shall we re-build this limping land?
Is it with stones, chromes & bones
or with rubble stones from tombs
                              and catacombs?
If we swallow wooden pestles
wont we perpetually stand erect?

If we anoint gun-men
as authorized breeders of brawls
wont they hand us scrolls to our bend,
                    to our end?
Yet these are mere mortals minding mortars
who can neither make things talk
                    nor make them walk

The slow, crafty one edges away,
deliberately so, he has left
ask *alii!*
His house of shell on his soft head
he eats soft mushrooms under dry leaves
while there he is asked two questions:
Can he who thinks he ought to put a knife to life
create life or cause it to flow or grow?
Can he who seeks to destroy this temple, rebuild it
even if we give him more days than three?

*Alii: name of Tortoise's wife in Igbo folklore.

OUR HATE

Each time, provoked, I toy with your throat
For reasons not far from tongue or tone
I've always heard behind us a loud guffaw
Oh fellow chasers of the gadfly & flea
Breaking fast on a menu of palm & kernels
You who'd embrace the brewers of our hate
Haters and loathers who hurt like vampires
Vampires like umpires who blow the whistle,
March to the periphery of the circle
And yet converge at the center

When they toast to the health of one another
We won't be there
When they sign contracts with their toes
We won't be there.

Yet you & me, blood knots to an eclipsed day
Are yet to learn the trick of dogs or cats at play
And would rather exchange brick & bat & clay
Brothers, our lot lies with nuts & palm nuts
So, let us fall in turn without the use of tongues
So we'd roll far ahead, away from the brink
Of their masterstroke—
                        the finger-pointing pranks of old

When they embrace before the camera
We won't be there
When they fly first class on London trips
We won't be there.

Yet you & me, lost between this huge arena
Of swamp & sand, nod to their fiesta fun

Of head-to-head knocks & cracks
When their erring buttocks are massaged
Brothers, look at me!
Whether you're of the flooded field
Or of the desert dune
Your face is as sour as mine
Sore
Spread with ash, rubbed of muck.
Children of my scattered fathers
Brothers who come from another mother
Can I whisper into your mishearing ears?
The shepherd will not dine with his sheep
Nor the slave-dealer with his luckless serfs
For all drovers speak the language of whips

> *When they plan to 'eye-mark' the cake*
> *We won't be there*
> *When they meet to share the loot*
> *We won't be there.*

So brothers, let us from now
                    do like the donkeys do
They'll prompt us to their polluted ponds
We shall padlock our mouths
                    to their deal of dung

ON THE ROAD TO DAMASCUS

On the road to Damascus one noonday
a midget of a man wore whips on his waist
and took on those he thought
were the apostates of his day
until he heard mysteriously behind him:
'Saul, Saul why do you persecute me?'
The offender was struck by a blinding bolt
And from the back, beyond his reach
he could not look up to see his tormentor
he having tormented the man's men to no end

For preaching against the mess of the age
for voicing the true message, message of truth
which the men insisted were far more superior
the short man pursued them with his whips
where Patriarch Moses crusaded tit-for-tat
these men preached forgiveness for all
where women were treated as inferior
the New Man reckoned with Martha
                    and the woman of Magdala
where a tribe thought it exclusive
                    to consult with the Above
to call on the name of the Mighty One,
                    and to look up in awe
the Sage said 'Oh no!' while writing on the sand
and assured all of entry to the Mansion Above
Of a truth he came for those spiritually sick
not for those who already had a visa
                    to the House Beyond
This was an abomination, an apostasy
in the eyes & ears of the tetrarchs of the tribe

who cried blue murder & chewed their hair
                                    in hate

Paul, still Saul, took it solely upon himself
to engage in a contest of will,
in a contest of bravura
with the focused followers of the salvaging sage
until a thunderbolt struck him from behind
and from his gilded sides he was dazed
From that day Saul became Paul
From that day he grew tall
From that day he parried the pall
From that day he blunted his sword
From that day he preached to the poor

Thereafter Paul's true call commenced:
five times at the hand of the tribe
he received forty lashes less than one
three times he was struck with rods
once he was stoned like Stephen was stoned
three times he was shipwrecked
when he passed a day, then a night on the sea
Endangered by floods and robbers
he travelled without stopping
denied himself many sleeping nights
in hunger & in thirst & in continuous fasting
often cold, naked in labor & hardship
and immeasurable discomfort & restlessness
What of detentions & imprisonments?
Oftentimes he was miraculously saved
What of beatings & frequent brushes
                        within the domain of death?
Mind you, the war with the word having ended
Paul embraced the word with a will

The war having ended indeed
he consumed the word with zeal

Yet as he dreamed to enter Damascus
the ethnarch called King Aretas
(he was the father-in-law of Herod Antipas)
lay in wait, bent like a boa intent to strike
or to a lesser degree to arrest & humiliate him
But Paul quoted the law: 'A judicial fact
shall be established only on the testimony
of two or three witnesses.'
You see that? Paul was a lawyer!

In all circumstances, imaginable & unimaginable
hold forth faith before you as you'd a shield,
he says, because this'll help you avert
                                  the fiery flings
from the wily one, the one who acts
without rhyme, without reason
Remember Demas?
He has left and taken off to Thessalonica
Cresens has gone off to Galatia,
and Titus to Dalmatia
The converted have only a companion in Luke…

Blessed are the advocates of hate in haste
They shall be converted!
Woe to the connoisseurs of bread in taste
They shall be dumbfounded!

AT THE BIRTH OF SNOW

At the birth of snow when the first glaciers
                    tangled with the surface of time
We were there wielding our axes daring the Alps
                    covered in snow

Before the Synagogue or the Italian church,
                    the Torah or the Bible
We patiently lay in wait in anticipation of the birth
                    of a Black Christ

During the fierce and roaring romance between Caesar
                    and Cleopatra
We were there because Caesar's comforter
                    was a whole-meal Negress

We erected pyramids with granite of stones
                    and stood them on the neighing Nile
We wrote art, wrote artifact, sidestepping atrocity
right on the somnolent stones of the Euphrates

We painted the sun & engraved stars of the sky
                    on the caves of Austria
Didn't we fight with Caesar's men, spank Spain
                    and pacify the Pyrenees?

Yet in the belly of the past, purposely pilfered history
                    lies comatose
Like a crested python which swallowed
                    what it shouldn't have touched

Do they still remember how the Moor-Africans
                    raided Europe on end?

Perhaps they have forgotten we are Othello's countrymen!
Perhaps they think the records are no more,
                            that history has been annulled!

These days, when I march through the seemly
                            streets of Sicily
I demand the African diamonds locked up
                            in those tall glass shops

These days, as I stroll into the British Museum,
                            extolled for its glimmers of myth
I ask the loquacious curator for our stolen symbols,
                            icons of greatness & might

These days, as I pass by Harvard Square
                and behold tramps in tortured eyes,
                children of *affluenza*
I demand the slave-labor which funded the cocaine pulls
                            in their bruised brains

MOTLEY WARS

NUCLEAR WAR

Nuclear war, nuclear war
For now forgotten after the unjust war
shelved away in the library of war-rest
awaiting mourning on the morning after
to be remembered again when a rebel roars
gas, gas-masks and all

May the tall tigers not provoke a nuclear tear
which quickly runs down the world's rheumy eyes
It will be fought back from secure gas chambers
If only we had learnt from the notes of Nagasaki!
Here, our masks are only those of *ulaga* and *ojïonu**
They are mere masks of art and artifice
not those of sci and tech

Techno lore now shows off large blade rotors
helicopters which practice maneuvers
like pondside dragon flies are wont to do;
they delight us as they march on water
like Apostle Pee imitating his wondrous master
But here we sink like a burdened stone
like the disciple without the requisite faith
Is this how we shall go nuclear?

Which rich man's cow & poor man's goat
graze on the same field at the same time?
Isn't it only trees with fruit that receive
                              clods of stones?
If a man bears no missile, bears no stick
nor swearwords in his frightened mouth
how does he intend to strafe a serpent?

If a man isn't too sure of his breakfast
Isn't he free to make bombs blast?

Postponed or not, nuclear war still hangs
Suspended in the air like a Chaka spear
pointing at the heart of a careless Earth
It is a deferred war snug in the gilded core

Nuclear war, nuclear war
Please, look at my sore!
When elephants tumble and pause
aren't the grasshoppers free to curse?

Ulaga and *Ojionu*: adolescent mask types among the Igbo, known for their singing and prancing about.

ROYAL SHELL MEETS KENULE

A hectic time it was, feisty if you ask me
being a season of warm, muggy weather
The white man, his face sweaty and tanned
pointed to the vat of palm oil in the hearth
Why not? the people reasoned
A loose change here, a pretty sum there
A little more than cowry shells & manilas
exchanged hands, white on top of black
One day the white friend lowered his gaze
after surveying the top of the palm tree
and trained it on the earth's bowel
like a *dibia** in quest of a child's *iyi-uwa***
He saw buried there barrels of gold in crude
Quickly he changed from prospecting
for the oil at the tip of the green palms
to lusting after the oil in the earth's crust
Why not? the people reasoned
The white man marched in the marsh,
marched in the mangrove
sent the swamps sweltering in stupor
and swore he would not pay!
The people raised their ear-lobes in the air
like a threatened rabbit would & watched
Then in his frenzy
the foreigner flung out his exploration organ
and urinated spills into the people's streams
discolored & upset the calm repose of rivers
defecated on the land refusing to flush
farted gaseous chemicals to foul the air
turned the alluvial soils into infertile sands
Yet the intruder's mission was not understood.

A wise man called Kenule, the people's Ken
rose in his diminutive height to ask questions
The prowler told them his name was Shell
a royal name from the royal realm
Still the white man was not understood
Then the impostor motioned at Government
Government motioned at Government *pickin*^{***}
richly clad in green garments of camouflage
who quickly handed out a few shells
to the stubborn villagers
After all, 'Who born dog'?
Meanwhile, shells in dynamites explode
in the background cracking rocks
to mean that the despoliation,
the desecration of the home soil must go on
Then Ken understood.

Such was the warmth of the day!
The man of the people, his brow full of sweat
sweated to know what next to do
He stood up to crow, stretched his full height
like a cock doing its bounden duty at dawn
A short man indeed, they cut his cockscomb
In short cut him to size, put him in prison
The villagers cried havoc,
raced into their backyards
and moulded maddened men into militants
who would burst pipes, search for the promise
that their pay-off was in the pipeline
not finding anything of value there
burst calabashes of oil wells in rigs
kidnapped whites of all tinge and tint,
asked for ransoms in greenbacks

raped some, black on top of white
and occasionally made them look heavenwards!

*dibia: Igbo traditional doctor.
**iyi-uwa: the tiny pebble said to be brought into the world by *Ogbanjes,*
children believed in Igbo cosmogony to die and quickly return, only to die
again. The concept of *iyi-uwa* is treated in Achebe's *Things Fall Apart* (1958).
***pickin: Pidgin-English word for child or children.

WAR ON TREES

At the descent of the green locusts
                which laundered our lawn
plundered, scrapped & emptied it
                into safe Switzerland safes
wanton want, octopal-shaped,
                paced our lachrymal land
and summoning strength barked
                at our trembling trees:
Why are you still standing there, towering in thrill
When bright brains in drains have left the land?

Imagine trees, proud icons standing
                at akimbo centuries on end
more or less pantheon of ancestral figures
                guarding the land
trees which earned revered places
                and were saluted as *Oke osisi**
Imagine ordering the trees of forked lanes
                on four heaths to leave!

Today I returned, I saw the land desolate,
                bare like an unfed orphan
recluse shedding orphan tears
Today the land has turned to mush,
                in places waterlogged
Erosion-prone as silky sands in sheets
                leave the land in a hurry

Galled, I sought to find out
                what could have gone amiss
how water entered the green pipes of the pumpkin
I'm told that some men in Mao suits came,

smiles on their small faces
                    our new masters in frail forms
whose aching eye-bags are now beginning to dry
                              of water
I'm told the gangling men,
always smiling in their small spectacles
are lovers, not of our warm women
                    waiting in Lagos whoretels
but our trembling trees, our *chlorofora excelsia,*
                    Oh the mighty iroko!

*Oke osisi: Igbo for a 'mighty tree'.

ONE SENTENCE

On this odd rung on the ladder of life
the twenty-one for that matter
on this winding stair of unfolding history
on this snaky stair-rail & route
a creed in our curious country
decrees death for a mere sentence
about beauty queens recalling
a messenger of the Ultimate King!
A Daniel* nearly faced judgment!
one dainty daniel
oblivious of the bobby traps of faith
in her bizarre country
scribbled a sentence, perhaps two on thisday**
this day *anno domino*
unfazed by the essence of the sixth sense
she missed a crucial step
on the winding stair of unfolding history
snaking away again before us like other centuries
altering colors like a chameleon
Needless to say she tumbled and crashed
and spilt a tensed moment on two hundred
with her ignorant parker pen in an experiment
spilling a fat-war on the permed hair of her head
A sour smell followed a trail of her race
as a farmer would on sensing
the devious darnel on his farm
Daniel vaulted over the ramparts of our realm
like a noisy fowl fleeing after fouling the air
You can see how prompt, how powerful
the prayer bead can be in our amazing country
or rather that which is claimed for creed
In our country, counters don't count

from naught, but from two hundred
Even two hundred human skulls count for little
for they aren't enough for the fops of force
to act, to brandish their batons yet
More so when such uncrowned heads
fall as offerings of a flaming faith
In our country, wilting under the weather
                    without the benefit of a first-aid
two hundred slain skulls
are not really priced
more than two hundred fish-heads
Even bonga, O yes bonga
has fishy rights activists fighting for her
fully in charge of sucking seasoned spare parts
of fish-heads & their prismatic eyes
                    in riverine resorts!

In our baffling country,
inebriate few though, they may say,
who pursue a creed of hate
a sentence of fate
primed their peppered eyes
at ahmadabad
aurangabad
hyderabad
islamabad...
you know all these *bad* places
and take their bearing from bad stances
Although the creed in a crescent
is a creed of ease, a creed of peace
some hoodlums, wild as Rottweiler
prance about piercing the hearts of fellow men
with soulless scythes & spears
and the breasts of women with sticks & stakes.

On this odd rung on the ladder of living
the twenty-one on the winding stair
                              of unfolding history
whose profit we may miss again
men who knew not what trufaith is meant to be
have turned tiny whispers, small sentences
with the Ultimate King
into a roar, then an uproar
Yet they claim they are doing the Great One great!

In our puzzling country
after every clangor on creed
after the stacks of scraps after rain
on the bigoted soils of our spoils
sultans of souls scribble one sentence:
'Our creed is lamb; bedlam is bad.'
Haven't the extremists heard that before?

---

*Miss Daniel, a journalist in 2002 then working for a Nigerian daily wrote
a scathing sentence which connected a revered figure in one of the faiths to
the Beauty Queens then visiting the country. Some fanatics of the said faith
coupled with hoodlums took the law into their hands, destroying buildings
and killing more than two hundred people for which no one was punished
until this day.
**The name of a Nigerian newspaper.

CAR WAR

This box of steel
dumb and still
can crawl or walk
or ride or run
if it is gently pressed
or comely caressed
furiously pushed
or recklessly shoved
Otherwise it can lie still
still in peace
still like unmoving steel
like a stillborn after labor
it can sit still
like a molded monument of old
looking at you
looking wherever you look
simply sit at a place
like any box of iron
or box of iron-and-steel
or of stone
it can be pushed to walk
or pulled to crawl
but haste will
neither
walk nor crawl
in the fluty honk of angry horns
in the thousand races of chaos
on Lagos streets
Haste will march it!
Haste will kick it!
Haste will depress it!
until the still box of iron

or box of iron-and-steel
or of stone
turns a ramshackle
box of blood
and bones
with four far-flung

bellies, far-flung
black & blue
of tyres burst
until some divine-deeds
precious creatures never found
or sold in superstores
of stocks & staples
are tossed far-off
like a shattered china
in the African sun
dripping with blood
and sweat from broken bones
and tones
tuneless
groan
moan
and growl
until someone who saw it
who felt it
filled with sense & commonsense
heaves
and sighs & says:
haste hoed this;
death harvested it.
Not forgetting the fury of the mob
that answereth by tyre!

COCCIDIOSIS, WAR OF THE WRYNECK

(to the seasonal *ogbulorie*,* the chicken ailment)

Coccidiosis, war of the wryneck
The scourge of my chickens
right in the mud kitchens
Is it true you too are death
On whom hangs my chickens' fate?
if death were your great grand sire
you must be his disowned heir!
If you're the dismaying death,
Can you strike humans dead?
Leave my harmless chicks alone
You who make them turn
and turn in sinuous curves
like the course of a laden stream
like in an *arenplane turner,*
*turn turn turner***
in the thought of your recurrent threat

Coccidiosis, war of the wryneck
Why unprovoked you
run after my little chickens
right into the mud kitchens
with all that agonizing pain
with all those sickly droppings of ash
sickened liquid dripping from their beaks
into their sacred little pens
where they shut their eyes
and they're not sleeping
and their breathing so noisy
doesn't indicate they're snoring?

Coccidiosis, war of the wryneck
You strike my chickens with paralysis
and assail their little minds with crisis
For making both of us mourn,
I declare you're nobody's chum
From the get-go cynics have been in doubt
if you were death's true offspring
If indeed you were
why do you sometimes miss your ware
and give the chick that dodges your dread
only a helicopter head?

Coccidiosis, war of the wryneck
Should you be the death we really dread
strike me today!
But I still prefer a propeller head!

*Ogbulorie: Igbo for the seasonal virus poultry disease, known in English as
coccidiosis.
**arenplane turner/turn turn turner: Igbo children's game of turning and twisting
in imitation of the manner enemy fighter jets turned and twisted in the air
during the Biafran war.

BIAFRA TESTAMENT

THERE, THAT'S THEIR BIAFRA

Wherever war has purred or whirred past
there, that's their Biafra,
there their world breaks out
like a peeping-tom of a sun in the morning
releasing rays of blood & marrows in bones
eyes reddened with rage query sacred quarries
Wherever war has purred & whirred past
the fate of families fills the air so foully
Whether it be the Battle of Britain
the War of Roses (Imagine war beside roses!)
or the Battle of Manila Bay, the Bay of Pigs
the fate of fools fills the air so fully
Not even the Battle of Okinawa should we gloss over
because here soldiers seeking to restore their roots
routed for romance in the rumps of comfort
women & whores
Wherever war has whimpered,
women waltz unto walls
on which weapons embracing weapons
try their tuff in hurls
Not even in Biafra where brothers dared
to throw *waka** at the other
could war be said to be warm or lukewarm
At Opi
the battle at Ugba
or that engulfing Nkpor
between Oba & Obosi
and in Abagana
the boom of doomed guns boomed
swallowed up stout-hearted soldiers in haste
on both sides of the bitter border-belch.

At Abagana
where recruits were routed in cannonade
the generals soon sensing things
                    were getting hotter
in furrowed faces quickly wrote their notes
                         in fury
fraternized with the wounded in a hurry
before announcing they were to take a flight
out of the tortured town
just to cart in more arms, not cartons of kiss
to end once and for all
the ding-dong affair for the enemy's throat
which they know have claimed deaths in droves
Howbeit they were escaping,
they were taking their inglorious exits
into the longing arms of their languid lovers
waiting on them on the bed-bugged beds
                         of cold misdeeds

War is not about notes, words or books of deeds,
about anybody's command at the rear of war feats
War is about scuds and swords intercepted by shields
which were often the bodies of men and women

Could war be said to be warm or lukewarm?

When B–26 sowed fear in the forest of moaning minds
in down town Warri
Sapele
Ore
and Okitipupa
men & women ran for cover
in trenches of treason
At Gakem, there landed a fifty-pound bomb

which dispersed traders at Obollo-Afor
At Orlu, the planes pandered to Uli
took leave in sordid somersaults
                           in the ominous air
headed for a hunch in the search
                           for an eluding peace
Here, did the war wane, did it end?
next was the pain, the pain to claim the peace
in a war food & food balls were used
to bring erstwhile brothers down on their knees
the battles, now multilayered,
refused to end there
they wore on, though nobody won the peace
on the shifting sands of a vexed victory
Thus from Gakem to Ugwunchara
from Opi Junction
to Ugba Junction
to Ahiara Junction of Ahiara Declaration
the battles wore on beyond 'police action'
in stubborn flanks and resistance pockets
like a dying man throwing up in throes

Where there were no guns anymore
or where bullets made gun-bearing
unwieldy
twigs came in handy
and so sticks
and stakes
and stones
and bones
from carrion-leftovers
That's why wherever war has whored or whirred past,
dock!
Because there things take a turn, then a tainted turn

Today, wherever men are cheated,
there that's their Biafra
Be it at the site of the damning dam of a Bakolori,
in the mangrove swamps of a beleaguered Bori
or when innocent girls are herded into a Sambisa

*Waka: Hausa abusive gesture with splayed hands at an opponent.

A KIND OF BIRD

A littlun in my little days in a little way
everything I then loved was little, so little
and leaped about lithe
O see little birds in bird wings perched on a peach
I lived with morsels of bird-joys
                        all of my little life
until this day & this morn
saw I another kind of bird
not so little though
not so fluffy either
nor like the birds preening their feathers
I saw in heedlessness as birds are wont to do

These weren't birds with fluffs
                        of feathers to unfurl
nor were they birds I knew cat-walked
                        in dainty steps
stealthily stealing maize seeds budded
                        in mama's stalks

This afternoon the sky was agog
                        with arks of sparks in flash
even of darts twinkling with a din
                        in a strange deal
Suddenly a descent of metallic birds
                        confronted the air
clangorous to hear whirr past tumbling,
                        poised to kill
their underbellies white as snow
                        in colorless chrome
They came quickly in morbid invasions
as by a trope of troops

Then I heard a clang, then a clangor
like those of a million benediction bells
or rather like the clank of metals
                    of heavy chains

Boom! Boom! Gwim! Gwim!

How come on this occasion a thing of beauty
is no more a form of fun forever?
How could birds I had known for their balm
                            and beauty
change to flights in fury, parceled out in frenzy?

Hastily we booted our way into bramble bushes
in time to secure our heads ahead of our lives
Right in the air, across the cross in the forlorn sky
the birds of war, birds all the same
strafed
coughed
and cursed
from branch, buttock & beam
and caused bullets to bring down destruction
on homes, hovels & homesteads
closing up pallid ponds & pondlets
Human blood freely flowed into floods
Fecal stuff forced out by fright flowed still
Human sweat, sour & salty conquered
our frightened little lips, into our littlun mouths
The foe has fought in mock doing his worst:
thatch huts without roofs
shredded bamboo beds scattered aloft
trees shed their bleached branches in great pain
rocks & sands, dry & wet, wait
scattered in spleen, in galls, in splinters

everywhere was calm
as if we'd entered a graveyard
not even chirps by crickets nor chicks cheeped
everywhere was smoke spilt in smoke-screen
bewildered eyes blotchy from fumes
soon spiral upwards
as if to report to a higher order
and like an exodus of refugees without a route
domestic animals ran in starts, halts & hitches

Life is a wonder if we observe it from under
After all a masquerade is not watched from a spot
Life is sweet if we can chew it in bits
How could a bird bear a belch in its bottom?
How could a bird, a beauty bit by bit
in the morning when it preens its fluff
as its behind quirked & quivered in glee
in nervous ecstasy, as if chartered to chatter?

In my little mind in my little way
weighed down by woe, I was to ask:
How could birds whose presence
gives me soul-kicks of charm
                    and enchantment
now having murdered their warbling calls
                    cause to kill?
Is a bird in the morning dew at the riverside
perched on a twig or perched on a peach
no more an exalted beauty born to behold?

KWASHIORKORED IN A WAR

In wars, it's not only bombs and bullets that kill
Hunger does, sorrow the same before shovels till

Kwashiorkored in a war, a war of virulent hate
Is one really better than death or even of fate?

Sallow, watery eyes lodged in sunken eye-sockets
Did we need to die from a hailstorm of rockets?

Ama's hair now soft and rusty like dry corn tassels
Didn't we see his feet encased in liquid muscles?

Those feet fought no war; war fought the feet owner
Fought Ama's mother; made his mother a mourner

Yet a sage, a wizard of our war, declared starvation
A genuine instrument to boost brotherly attrition

Who made Ama this way?
Who denied Ama his May?
Made his belly bloated with air, runny?
Made his sickly bottom flattened, bony?

I saw many an Ama on the battlefronts of Biafra
Just as they also fumbled in the fields of Eritrea
Plagued by kwashiorkor on the turf of Ethiopia
Wasn't it the same in the theatre of Somalia?

What have we planted on this land?
Bomb & bomb blast?
Or bread & breakfast?

IN THE GLARE OF THAT LIGHT

In the glare of that light
I saw the desire for frog-leaps
to feather selfish nests
brew unsettling isms,
saw egos brew hate, brew schisms

In the glare of that light
the light of our tripped trip-flare
you saw bullets
you saw bayonets
you saw bullets & bayonets
beckon to a blunderbuss

In the glare of that light
we saw the sores of Warsaw
we saw the flies of France
we saw the vultures of a vassal state
Flies saw the sores first
but vultures arrived faster than the flies
Anyway, both feasted on the open flesh

In the glare of that light
frogs took their leaps
nests got festooned with feathers
isms schemed to plant schisms
egos echoed the dream of dread
but wandered in the lawn of peace

Now look no farther afield,
you'll see our sons settled in Oji*
    scary dry scares all over
    flesh bearing bone-deep bullets

thigh-stubs morbid like tree stumps
scarecrows clutching crutches
wheel-chairs driving man-child
artificial legs compelled into a make-up
deaf ears which hear only drums of the dead
blind eyes which only see a chance by trance

*Oji River is a town in Enugu State where wounded Biafran war veterans
have been domiciled since after the Nigerian Civil War.

AN EYE FOR THE UNSETTLING

BOMBLAST OR BREAKFAST?

i.

In the fullness of the never-hurrying time
which the poor of my land enjoy aplenty
it seems the predictions of the men of old
                              still endure
those men with their prescient eyes
trained at the desert, trained at the forest
saw icicles of truth blurred by bubbles
                              in the oases
equally hidden in the forests
adorned with a wooded hedgerow

ii.

aren't bombs now the major on our menu?
aren't bloody loaves of unleavened bomb
what make our human tables of hunger tick?
My forefathers endlessly fought flames of fire
over fertile lands in a forest
                    of a thousand fireflies
but these were innocuous internecine wars
often wars of regeneration
marked by the loss of a few folks
during which they cast off their sloughs
like those of pie-eyed pythons lodged
in the bole of the bold *iroko*
just to refurbish their dwarfed world
yet by then they bombed
not like these days though
anyway they were not bomb-scared either
after all bombs flew off their entrails
when they could not help it

like would fly off their mouths bombs of curse
when their erring wards questioned their wisdom
then men were men
and their women, strong, sincere, full of sense
knelt down on one knee
to welcome the prime-time palm wine
offered by their pragmatic
but not-so-romantic husbands

iii.
then war was not a distant paradigm
it did not hang in the air like *akuko-na-egwu*˟
then we couldn't guess if the clamor had armor
it wasn't like the eating of a breakfast of dread
with the devil thus occasioning
                        the use of a long spoon
If it was proper to eat with the ugly one at all
why did the angels throw him down,
                        down the throne of abyss?
Couldn't the rotor-winged ones afford long spoons?
My people, masquerade is man;
only profit makes him spirit!

iv.
Indeed war was not like scolding an anaconda
from a distant spot of safety
because we can only tell the lion
he's a greedy animal from afar
in the forest of doubt or dread
then men with wet pepper in their eyes
on both sides of the offended divide
clasped with each other in a fiery grip

muscle for muscle, tense & taut
while their spectators, comrades-in-clasp
egged them on not too far
                    from combatant & kin

v.

today the artillery man,
                    behind him a bombardier
full of fright hides under a canopy of shrubs
fires blindly from the security of his leaky lair
like an old man whose two young wives
                    are engaged in fisticuffs
who can only shout, "What's the problem?"
from the safety of a fearful distance
because his loin-cloth, fickle, flighty
threatens to fall off his withered waist

vi.

a war-lord sits on the throne in televiv
glued to a radar, more or less a tv
he directs the muzzle of war & war-heads
at babeling bagdad
dull-in-the-brain dads,
not dull-in-the-crotch though
whose first love is war
'cos they were born in war & would die in war
with leaky bags & vats of courage
armed with bare balls of scorns & stones
declare the mother of all wars
                    only on wounded lips
and lay claim to feats of catching
                    flying scuds in the air

fathers, preys of war, victuals of war
kiss the earth with thuds of hoofs of death
firmly posted on their sweaty backs

mothers their babies backed
                    where bullets berth
undertake a strange exodus of a thousand
and one milestones scampering for safety
where for unrequited years,
                    years of sorrow & torment
they'd have to be Internally Displaced Persons
where they'd have to cook anemic meals
                    on three stones,
on improvised hearths of disease & death
in conc camps, their babies posted on their backs

vii.
God watches men's idiocy & chortles
(His white beard quivers)
as the folly of men frequently unfolds
and we complain He does not care a hoot
Isn't it how the zebra runs its stripes?
Is a chortle not a chuckle?
Is it not a kind of care, a kind of repair?
Doesn't He know a baby is better
                    than a bomb?
Isn't it why we are delivered of babies,
                    not of bombs?
He knows as well that a barrel
of
break
fast
rather than a rumble

of
bomb
blast
can feed the never-fed fold
and tackle the tantrums of loveless men
who with pepper in their hazel eyes
feed on transferred blame,

                on hastened aggression

viii.
today the war-lord & the war-witch
prefer bombs thrown from the aerial zone
shattering fields & yields at home
with sharp shrapnel of gall mixed with guilt
today bombs issue from the anuses
of jet-lagged jets and burnished bombers
though not like the simple farts
from the tired buttocks of our unhurried fathers
today bomb blasts compel men & women
children & toddlers, princes & bastards
to scamper for their souls from a furnace of hatred

ix.
when a bomb blunders into ocean depths
who knows what fishes & mollusks
may think about their restless neighbors?
When a hauled Molotov from a distance
lands on the surface of the sea
do we surmise
oysters
crabs
and clams

are amused?
If bombs visit farmlands
cassavas crawl into ant-holes
of the anthills of hunger
yams which may have sprouted
                    their tender tendrils
wither away
their dry leaves dotting the land
like the failed independence flags of fatherland

x.

a bomb
lands
on the dining table of a throaty mound
round and rotund
like that mythical mount of meal
where things have fallen apart
such that diners close enough
                    for kiss on both sides
may not see the godly twinkles of love
in the pain-filled eyes of fellow men
often what is seen are the twitches of hate
often what emerges is the revolving
                    sprocket of fate
from father to son, from son to siblings
often what is heard are the curses
which jump out of frustrated mouths
what is inhaled is the smoke of fleeing
metallic fowls headed for the unbounded air
like a hawk beaking up a chick
                    or the unlucky lizard
instead of the scent of *foo-foo*
                    and its accompanying soup

what is torched is another man
with flesh
with blood
as if he were a log of wood
with a cankered cortex and pith
in concentric rings of rot
fit for felling
or forever snuffed out as the Savior decreed
against the never-yielding fig tree
what leaves a taste in the mouth
is not the French *etuvée* nor her *jambon*
but the tang of our fireside dang
in a rough dough of anguish, suffering
and pain & yet a piss of pain

xi.
We must now ask the bomb-maker
or the death-maker for that matter
if bombs can cater
for our breakfast & brunch
Shouldn't we ask the bullies of Oregon or Utah
about those moaning underground mills
making arses of men with barns of arsenal
to extinguish life, extinguish love?

xii.
if bullets may hang round our necks
and we still go to bed hoping to earn a sleep
can we ask the pilots of aversion in the aerial zone
if the shrapnel of their explosives
those large, lurid eggs of metal
may feed the multitude of men

like it was on five loaves & two fish,
not counting women & those yet to be weaned
let us ask the artillery man
hunched behind his bazooka platform
if those cannon balls he blindly pumps into air
may serve as Italian pizzas
on the tables of a hungry humanity

akuko na egwu is Igbo for folksong, now generally used for a made-up story, a fabrication.

THE BOMB-MAKER

i.

The bomb-maker is a death-maker
because at the wedding of wilt & wail
the bomb-maker is the cake-maker
he is the cook for the spooks
the halo in the abyssal hollow

ii.

in the grocery of harm
the bomb-maker is the caretaker
There ingredients
abound:
vial of hate & hatred
gall & gall-bladder
gun & gun-powder
fire & wire
nail & shrapnel
bullet & pellets
plug & slug
bar & ball
dynamo & duel
rack, muck & ruin
on
doomsday

iii
bomb-maker
do you really have kinsfolk?
Have you ever sat with your folk men
in exchange of tender thoughts?

Did you serve them the cocktail
in a Molotov cocktail?
What of a father?
has he called you to a morning meet
to a morning repast
about your future and your pleasure?
do you mean you have a mother?
As a baby
did you suck her matter
I mean her breasts for milk?
As a baby
did she clean your nostrils of mucous?
As a baby
did you ever chuckle in her mothering arms?

iv.
bomb-maker
do you have a wife?
have you ever been tickled by her thighs?
or are you married to steel, alloy & all?
Is iron-bar your father-in-law?
and anvil the mother of your wife
who is your sister?
a shyster or a trickster?
Is brutal your brother
or caustic your cousin?

v.
Perhaps, you have fatal for father
murder for mother
and chills for children

vi.

For sure, the bomb-maker
is a death-maker
at the crowning of the cruel Cain
the bomb-maker was the king-maker
the viper hidden in the veil of violence
the sorrow in the attic hollow

vii.

bomb-maker
at another birth
death shall be your berth
at your reincarnation
there shall be no incantation
at another birth
your bomb shall be dumb
and your mortar mute
the balls of your scrotum
shall serve as metal balls
your flesh the flint
your penis the plug
your shit the shrapnel
your intestines the wire-lines
your shattered brain a shell of fire

viii.

bomb-maker
do you have our blood?
red & rare to fake or clone?
do you have a heart?
bean-built & brittle to break?
do you really have a soul?
Oh! All those thunders & toll!

MAN OF WAR

How could one be sure
        of where he was coming from
or of what use he could still possibly be?
Howbeit, at the Schipol, the busy
        bee of Holland
Man of war was delayed and de-pistoled
and left with a sick suit & a swagger-stick
Now virtually a hot air,
isn't one battlefield's trash
a desperate war-lord's treasure?
So he looked Africa-wards, the home of hostilities
        and proclaimed martyrdom
Tall & tawny & scrawny, a can-do
with sunken eyes & sunken cheekbones
his black beret perched on his receding hair
like the skullcap of the absent-minded bishop
Man of war may have crossed seven seas
abandoning his calm & comely clime
traversing glaciers, snowflakes & wet sands
to die for me in the season of scarce saints

I've died in Cambodia before
on the side of Kama Rouge
In Sri Lanka
I died for the Tamil Tigers
I've thrived in Mogadishu
For a while a specter in Bosnia,
in the Taliban tango in Afghanistan
I berthed in the Battle of Benghazi,
Quaddafi's quandary

I want to fight for you, fight your foe,
die for you
he declares even as the gun-holster
                on his waist is empty
His eyes slide sideways like a dog's
                        targeting a piece of fried fish
His collarbones depressed,
                they could hold a glass of vodka

In his head
death tolls insistent earth-calls
Etched in his side-pockets are lines of fortune
In his hands, his open arms, that is
death throws a precarious halo
I want to fight for you, fight your foe,
die for you
But in the brain scheme of the man of war
cash is sketched in shekels, marks & pence

then ranks rankled:
now a captain
then a major
three weeks a colonel
in three months a Brig
Sometimes the promotion of one man
declared desperately needed in the felling
field of men
in Eritrea
Liberia
Sierra Leone
or dr Congo
pours dogs & cats
like an African rain in the middle of July
All this hassle just to obtain the expertise

of one man
who has a diploma in death,
versed in dread!

Man of war, fight for me
Man of war, die for me
die for your talents
die for your silver
much more than thirty

BABY SOLDIER

i.
Stuck to the teat
of a bottle feeder
surely life cannot be sweeter
the nipple
fountains with milk
caresses the teeth
caresses the tongue
the little boy runs a runny nose
at each of his eye-corners
eye-feculence, butterish, stick
like a clip of fate
But they still snatched him away
from the quivering teats
of his mother's bare breasts

ii.
Little Lasanah thought it was fun
when they presented him
with what appeared in his little eyes
like a toy
on the fields of Buchanan & Bo
with the reverence of a precious present
he held it
It was a slim, sickly stick
though bearing a wondrous weight
His mother had bought him
something like that before
a thing which had made him
gulp a glass of a life-time of joy, a toy
as he laughed ear-to-ear

but this one was different
mother's gift was far too light
far too bright, far too filled with fun
This one on his shoulder is demon dark
far too cold, far too stiff
It is a *Kalashnikov*
bearing a pointed mouth of death
like a monster of a few nodes,
like the ogre
in grandma's bedtime tales

iii.
Whether light, weighty or wet
each pops a sound
with a trigger-touch,
one raises the feet of children
to marvel
and to giggle
one gets the birds scampering away
wondering how funny
cruel kids can be
the other
hauls a man into the air
and returns him to earth
with a sturdy stud of thud

iv.
To the baby soldier
of a mourning monrovia
this is baffling fun!
how can a pop of sound
make a man lie still?

how can a pop of sound
make a man shut his eyes?
how can a pop of sound
make a man forget to say goodbye?

v.

This is not like my
plastic bottle-feed
abandoned at home
which at a pressure-touch
issued a little quaff of milk
which caresses my teeth
cuddles my tongue
soothes my throat

vi.

Having found out
that a stick of steel
can pop a sound
and a man lays still
Little Lasanah holds the metal ware
aloft
When plucked
as in a box-guitar
twangs
cackles
and crackles
From a distance,
in his infant's mind's eye
he observes
the exposed teats
of his mother's abandoned breasts

beckon,
call on him to suck life
but duty calls
with the imperious command
of a death very much due
a duty to maim & to mangle
a duty to raid & to rape

vii.
On the fitful fields of Freetown
siblings
are forgotten
foams of baby babble
burst
on breastboobs
the slate of abc is bartered
for a metal ploy
the steely silly stick
now his pall & pal
slung
over his slim shoulder
he now throws his drunken gait about
like a midget rigged in as a giant god
on whose shoulders
life
and death
perch precariously
like a decorated
general after a war he never won

viii.

One day

*katakata** claimed the clans of Kakata

a shot suddenly fires itself

or so it seemed indeed

Kpoooo!

Before little Lasanah

a man lay still

He hears a questioning voice behind him:

Did you kill?

No

That's your gun, isn't it?

Yes

It's barrel is hot.

Yes it is warm

Did you aim the rifle?

Yes

Did you touch the trigger?

Yes

Did you kill anybody?

No

What then happened?

The man

just

fell

down!

*'Katakata' is the Nigerian Pidgin English word for crisis or trouble.

FAMILY FISTICUFFS

1

Old Inyama, the yam farmer
thought he was such a man!
Who in his place wouldn't?
a man worth three wives
and fifteen mouths as he'd say it
must celebrate his manhood
with a frozen face
and muscular mien
among his women
and the many mouths he fed
a man worth a yacht of yams
must beat his breasts in boast
This is a man other men
seek to engage his eyes
a man of plenty
a man of estate & airs

2

Bomboy, a big boy, was born
when old Inyama served in Bombay,
     a Bombardier
during the white man's second big war
Imagine the boy's name: Bomb-boy!
or where Inyama served: Bomb-ay!
or the rank he wore: Bomb-ardier!
Surrounding old Inyama were bombs!
What a pleasure it gave the great Bombardier
when his second wife gave birth to a boy
weighing a great weight levered down
as an introductory poundage on planet earth

a world in which the weightless

                 count for naught

and men with obese weight throw it around

scatter their bulbous buttocks

              as they dawdle about

like elephants in hurried trundles

to catch up at the hint of fresh fronds & lotus

                3

Bomboy asks for his school fees

Old Inyama runs his eyes up & down his bulk

as if a rope has been mentioned

in the home of a failed suicide bidder

he spits once, spits twice

and asks the bubbly boy if his mother

pays school fees for all the lessons

he has taught her all these past years

Bomboy's mother only hears 'your mother'—

she knows it'd never be in praise—

Sparkles of blue murder

flew out of her eyes as in an impassioned slap

leaving her breathless & enervated

What did you say, Inyama?

the old yam farmer,

his fists quickly form a bunch

like one desirous of a punch

throws some yam seedlings at Bomboy's mother

marking a kick-off of the combat

Incensed, Adanta aims a blow

               at her teaser's jaw

Chineke mie!* Who taught this woman

              how to throw punches?

Adanta withdraws tactically & comes again

This woman will kill me o!

yells the yam farmer as he struggles
with his loose loin-cloth
See her formed fists set for war!
*Umunna eeh!*** Tell her to abandon
her boxing brawn, especially her left hook
In a flash old Inyama is on the ground
struggling with his wilted waist-cloth
If you won't pay Bomboy's school fees
who will? Adanta asks
did I impregnate myself?

4

Inyama's third wife intervenes
but before their husband could say
'Face them!'
his youngest wife is on the dust
her wrapper parting into two

Old Inyama dusts his buttocks
so conscious of *agbisi****
and withdraws to his leaky hut
Of what use is a local man of means
whose roof leaks in rain
who can't pay his son's fees
whose loin-cloth looses at will?
Of what use is a yacht of yams
if its harvester hoards such a harvest?
Of what use is the one called Bomboy
if he can't bomb the father's new wife
and teach her a lesson of her life,
being the order in a family of multiple mates?
This third wife who has just come
to reap where she had not sown
this intruder who has just invaded

the homestead of a wealthy yam farmer
who is muddled
maudlin
miserly
and mean
who wants to live the rest of his life in style
with a sweet-sixteen
Bomboy soon acts out his name
With one hand
he grabs his father's sulking sixteen
and casts her into the bovine dung-heap
formed out of Inyama's goats & sheep

        droppings
There the new girl cries helplessly in a dungeon
and so her new-born babe from its forlorn cot

    5
Old Inyama much aware that he is no longer
      a Bombardier
having lost his ability to bomb his adversaries
merely peeps through the palm-sized
window of his hardy hut
like a tortoise out of its shelter of shell
all he can do is sigh
and remind the plump boy
that he was once like him

    6
Everywhere is silent
No neighbor has turned up
to ask what has gone wrong
They are used to the daily drama
in Bombardier's action-filled domain

7

Old Inyama raises his voice & calls out:
Umunna eeh! Have you all gone to sleep?
Adanta & her son want to kill me o!
When no help comes, when no kinsman turns up
Inyama gives up hope & gives himself up

8

Adanta, with my permission, have a free rein
Take me whole & entire
Turn me inside out like a bag of yams
to be displayed at the *Nkwo* market square!

*Igbo for 'O my God!'
**Igbo for 'My kinsmen!'
***The floor ant dreaded by children for its painful sting.

THE DANCE IN DARFUR

1.

Darfur like the famed *UFOs* of the fifties
is chewed over in snippets of slow whispers
to a never-waking world
Between sleep & wake
bbc intones in the morning so early o'clock
...And in the war-torn region of the Sudan
You hear this like a refrain so early o'clock
even as one lounges under a blanket fur
about a land lying prostrate called Darfur
where farms & grazing fields burn like sulphur
where lives & property evaporate like camphor
where livestock, sickly, an obvious eyesore
ruefully march drunkenly like Lagos *danfo*
on city routes filled with rabid holes of yore
zigzag their way as if wonky with weed
It's about the *abid*
and the *zurga*, inferior from crib
the *janjawiid* going after them
armed with canons of creed & greed

2.

But the world tipsy with talk
Holds talks, yet more talks
about what to do with the Strong Man of the Sudan
who clad in a white turban bearing a swagger stick
stokes the fires of faith
and hate burning up his countrymen
What has *ICC* got to say today?
How many broken promises will fill with fruit
an empty basket strung round with false hope?
Yesterday the man with a bandaged head

sharing out wounds like panadols in a sick bay
had a noon bash, basking in Kenya
and quickly returned to his fortress
in his curious capital called Khartoum
Why couldn't Mwai Kibaki put a wedge, why?
Ocampo asks, sounding smugly resigned
The Big Man swings round in his consuming suit!
Being an economist,
Mwai chooses to be economical with the truth
and draws an occulted blank,
his eyes filled with soot

3.
That's how all these years El-Bashir, in sheer bravado,
unabashed bashes the heads of the Darfurians
That's how he manages to shine in the dance in Darfur
where men roughing the udders of their cows
as they search for milk to sip or suck
are themselves riffled, burnt as in barbecue,
where women, a sorority in suffering
like livestock leave in fleeing feet,
Soon they realize
that in a drunken journey without direction
haste has no meaning
All they do is long for life, just long for life
seated on a bitter flower hedge
look forlorn
at the furnace of fire burning their land
the toes of their toddlers sticking out
like little tired tortoises
lying in ambush waiting for unwary worms
Homeless girls not knowing what to do
do what next presents itself
wanton boys growing up in anger & danger

mature in haste & bear arms
whose workings they hardly know.
They were the kids of yesterday
forced off their mothers' breast teats
at the point of a gun
And who have since learnt to ape & to rape!

4.
Darfur, like the famed UFOs of the fifties
is retold and retailed in hushed whispers
to a not-so-caring world
It is what the voa wakes us up with
so early in the morning
...And in the Darfur region of the Sudan
You hear this like a refrain so early o'clock
even as one lounges under a blanket fur
about a despoiled land called Darfur
where land mines are now yam tubers
and gun-powder the people's *farine de manioc*
where bullets, like seed yams,
whir past like hailstones
of the African thunderstorm
in a dubious type of winter
where roofs forcefully take their leave
and doors fling open, broken
usher in a volley of shots
posted by irate Kalashnikovs
cornered by some careless kids
certain camels with uncertain loads on their backs
wobble like thrashed thieves
on the way to their own Calvary
on the tarmac where cauldron holes
decorate the land like weird ornaments
and birds only sing their swan songs

5.

On air, tuned only for a few ears to hear
the displaced, homeless, grim-faced, dour
sored, sullen, hungry & unbathing
bear their little transistors on their shoulders
They hear the bbc, voa, radio france etc
spread the gimmickry of humanitarian aid
of how lives were saved & lost
with a little more hunger, some
parched throats & tired urine!

A BOKO BOMB

A Boko bomb is my country's
sole claim to sci-and-tech!
Formed from the froth of faith
at the prompting of a power pose
served on a platter of spiced pudding
Formed from the fangs of filth, from cant & kill
from the humdrum of humbugs
on the querulous corridors of hate & hurt
of noise, injustice & disorder
a Nigerian bomb ought to be peppery indeed!
Being produced from the industry of greed
always gathering, gathering
with wires of wiles against the weak
in a do-or-die, in a you-die-or-you-do
from the rust & crust in tombs
a Boko bomb is the surest route to a catacomb.

In a land the biguns guzzle anything in sight
and like ants spirit the rest into Swiss holes
in fulfillment of the gospel of the Day-of-Rain
for their bomb babes yet to be born
where nothing is left for the ash-lipped ones
Not even a frosty slime of stew or spew
where worn-out babies merely sigh & cry
simply destined to die upon their birth
What the tiny tots of the poor chanced on coming
wasn't what their embryo brains thought at arrival
nor had prepared them to meet in their tiny cots
See, tiny babes, your country produces bombs:
They are our catch-up in sci-and-tech!

With pomp
occasionally encased in aplomb
the Nigerian bomb is bitter, pain-filled
made out of tombstones
which thunder had struck
plucked from the plaster cast
of deceit & defeat
from the free-flowing blood or flood
killed for arbitrary reason
in a contrived country,
far from what was thought
where few are now that country,
Having turned the land upside down
like bats would do at night
where buzz bombs wouldn't locate them
where many graze in dells of hell
                              and the faceless,
forceless, tongue-tied stand in jail

FIVE HAIKUS
FOR HOLLOW MEN
AT THE HELM

THE BOAST

I'll join the army
To hear songs in front of wars
Mother, do I join?

QUESTION TIME

Foreign help is fine
General sir, what of aids?
I beg your pardon!

PEACE-SAKE

Disarmament talks
Enthused, the General signs
A gun on his waist!

FOOTNOTE

Listen, you traitors
The right of my Human Right
Dreads the active Left!

MACHIAVELLI'S WHISPER

To marry the Throne
Macbethize fellow plotters
O Life-President!

TO THE HEEDLESS ONES

CUCKOROROCOO!

Cuckororocoo!
Cuckororocoo!
Cuckororocoo!
This is no cry occasioned by cough or hic-cough
It is not a screech of a bird troubled by leeches
It is the ranting of angst, the cry of anguish

Cuckororocoo!

At the cry of a crowing cock—
the unpaid town-crier of our clan—
the wise rise to recover debts,
bake bread or simply upset their beddings

Cuckororocoo!

This is the cursing call of the troubadour
in the morning, so early o'clock in the morning
Is anyone listening!
Nobody.

Cuckororocoo!

It's only a song! Doesn't Dan Maraya sing?
Now at the sound of their not-so-useful songs
I'll deploy my kinsmen
                    at the door of the armory

Cuckororocoo!

Seismic songs are made of these
The Egrets of our colonial past knew it,

                                  dreaded it
Our own cows prefer hemlock
                        to the coos of cockatoos

Cuckororocoo!

Yet from the triangular head of a bold beak,
Comes the universal song of the red cockscomb
                        of red hair & red beard
Isn't it funny that even cocks wear red,
                                the badge of bards?
We wear a black hair, black beard, black mouth,
                                a plaintive voice
Yet never will we try a cry of cuckororocoo.

Cuckororocoo!

At night the cock is a solitary figure, no company
But in broad daylight it is cocksure of a consort.

                                Cuckororocoo!
                                Cuckororocoo!
                                Cuckororocoo!

SOLDIERS LOVE OIL

Soldiers love oil; of course they do!
But on their stern & creased countenance
no trace of oil at all
you'll only know they love oil
when you see them devour roast yams
soaked in palm-oil, salted in pepper
and in the frenzied field of fight
oily soldiers snap
being furious foot-soldiers at battle
where brawn always wins

At the battle for oil
at the rigs they've rigged
soldiers sweat, slither & slip
because at such a battle
only muscular men matter
As fire-flames consume self-allocated wells
so men, their guns slung over their shoulders
leap off clearly from parade grounds
and head for the armory in their souls
to seize the door to the armory of corporal power
which had always oppressed their persons

Their first victims are usually the civilians
whom they dare call bloody to their faces
for being idle-brained, for being the bourbons
who hardly learn nor hardly forget
because they've never laid on their stomachs
in the forest of a thousand explosions
because they've never fought
                              to unite their country

because they've never promised, even glibly
by lip-service to pay the supreme sacrifice

Years later, dressed in *agbada* & *shokoto*,
                          a cap to match
soldiers return to power after wielding guns
because after all come what may
old soldier never tires, never dies
unless he knowingly hits his head on a stone
Now adorned in a bloody civilian dress
egged on by the man living on Mount Minna
Like a tortoise would always peek out of his shell
or like a fox stalks wild fowls in the forest of silence
the man on the hill who lives
in the House on the Hill in Minna or thereabout
pisses down causing smoke to rise to his abode
Below a long line of young generals in new attire
often taught to be tired, then retired at thirty-five
cast their eyes above like the Israelites
                          awaiting Manna
and then as in a parade file out like soldier-ants
their faces relaxed in a mock smile
                          face the Rock in Aso
These days every election year is a thuggery year
Retired soldiers, remembering what oil tastes like
go for the gubernatorial shields in their states
or else militarily march into parliament
where they turn sin-ators or representathieves

Soldiers love oil; of course they do!
They were trained by caning
eyes bloodshot, a prelude to glaucoma
they were caned to be crazy, crowned
to crow & bark as bullies bark

Isn't that why the democracy
we practice is known as *demoncrazy*?

See what oil can do in a country, to a country
nobody knows what to do with the oil money
as once claimed by a soldier statesman
Is that why we suck the oil but care less
about the environment, shedding only oily tears?

Is that why all the refineries are on forced holiday?
Is that why we now drive & fly on imported fuel?
Is that why everyday in every week, now & then
petroleum products enjoy hikes in their prices
because sleaze has since taught our leaders
what can be done with the oil money?

Can they then rinse their mouths
with cups of crude to kill the germs
trapped at the root of their rotten gums?
Can we ask them to bathe with oil, to rub oil
to remove the *craw-craw* on their sloughing skins?
Can we ask them to toast with a tot of premium spirit
the spirit that informs the nature of their type of democracy?

TOOTHED LORDS

(for African dictators, military & civilian)

Toothed lords, grand lords of the meek & the minor
Armed to the teeth, proud inheritors of tongues of fire

Where the rest of us are fall guys, damn flaccid fools
Much afraid to hold jack-knives or cause graphic pulls

Toothed lord, clad in the legendary King Midas gear
Everything you feel or touch turns into iridescent gold

Blessed are those whom you once copied from in class
Their pale pockets shall soon be lined with dry tapioca

Toothed lord, often accompanied by a trade-mark grin
Is that a gap in your teeth or did you carve it yourself?

I see that you see the rest of us as flabby figurines
Fit for flattening by decrees, by parliamentary pukes

I see that your feculence now issues in metallic lumps
And your urine a long stretch of copper-coated cable

So even if storms in weather are brewing in the air
Your umbrella of rainbow is cast a marble parabola

As for the croco & the hippo bathing in our streams
Let the hungry sharks be their children's nannies!

Toothed lords, grand lords of the meek & the minor
Armed with the famed fangs of the devious Damocles

You've learnt to silence our thin lips of shrill songs
With one thrust of steel fingers across our straw slits

What of signs of raw steams, storms of the oppressed?
Rain-chasers stand by, armed with phials of gun-powder

Much wiser now, I know the sword can do just anything
It can smother the stubborn; it can scribble signatures!

Toothy lord of the jagged grin, mad Lord of the Manor
Mama wonders what crime she may have committed

Don't forget, her 'illegal' structure fed your bulldozers
And Papa having lost his job, Junior had to quit school

After those 'economic' measures, what's Junior doing
At night when his mates breast their beds to sleep?

For now, more hands should join our feeble forces
To dispel the dew in the firmament of our crosses

Don't you ever think mayhem is exclusive to May?
The 'ember' months are famous for road mishaps

WHAT DO WORDS WORTH?

When blundering bullets shattered Sharpeville
But for words, the world settled for a sleeping pill

When biased bullets slaughtered a sulking Soweto
But for tirades, the world stood with arms akimbo

Daily the world stands supine like the red cockscomb
While brother bosses turn our soils into our catacomb

Year after year the AU is resolving on these raw deals
But really it's like it's revolving on nursery cog-wheels

"This time we shall be firm on certain crucial questions."
Let us hail countless resolutions devoid of actions!

Come rain, come shine we shall grope for you,
AU, allow me to ask you: Where are you?

At your usual annual ritual configured as a meeting
In which emissaries hauling portfolios are feting?

Toasting scarce Champaign and Scotch-on-the-Rock
Never in a hurry to press the boils on our hard buttock

Preferring to address newshounds in airport lounges
Muttering those now-familiar & memorized nuances

Like fratricide, suicide
Plebiscite, genocide…

You know, simply recounting those grievances of old
Waiting for true freedom to come on a platter of gold

Hoping *all* countries would soon obey the UN Charter
A charter which has charted the course of mere chatter

A matter we know a *fontomfrom** of words cannot fund,
For what are words worth if they lack shape or form?

*Fontomfrom is the sound of a Ghanaian drum-type, popularized in the
poetry of Atukwei Okai.

SEVEN GREAT MEN

This year, they will meet again in a cold room
to exchange notes in pinch-your-nose monotone
to eat & pick their teeth on sedate seats
with timed clicks of their tainted tongues
in tinkling laughs
they'll gather again in the annual ritual
of civilized row
about their savior role in a world
of both weal & woe

Seven great men
on the dead man's chest
Ho! Ho! Ho!
they'll cure him of his cough!

Bowler hats worn to cover fading hair
over pressurized hearts in machined acts
adorned in breeches & blazers
walking-sticks welded in casts of steel
costly coats & cuff-links in gold
prized shirts, suits & shoes
bearing etched designs & tell-tale tattoos
gold-plated teeth
artificial lenses of invented eyes
faces, spiteful, spiked with cauterized smiles
Just seven!

Seven great men
on the dead man's chest
Ho! Ho! Ho!
they'll cure him of his cough!

In their ritual cold room, noise-proofed
of double-speak & double-squeak
of fair trade mantra & seasonal fair
of hide-and-speak on arms & armed lords
of speak-and-hide on select injustices
the doors open & squeak
provoked by sylphlike diplomatic corpses
in remembrance of broken promises
of a hope ago
Here they are seated, sated with pleasure
of luscious shades in lush décor
tooth-pick & all

Seven great men
On the dead man's chest
Ho! Ho! Ho!
they'll cure him of his cough!

Here they are gathered again
like gods do gather to sip in snippet-sips
the world's solvent of sorrows:
terror
disease
flood
tsunami
mother-to-child disaffection
sorry, mother-to-child infection?
Then sermons about the seven powers
claiming seven is heaven
Who built the house called greenhouse
filled with carcasses clothed in gangrene?
What about aids from maids
hunger resting on cliff-hanger
famine farmed out to mines & booby-traps

climate eternally changing & changing
Isn't global warming global warning?

Seven great men
on the dead man's chest
Ho! Ho! Ho!
they'll cure him of his cough!

The seven men are gods gathered
at a calm concourse in a cold room
deodorized of humdrum siege on their seats
full of smiles in backslaps
ear-to-ear
eyeball-to-eyeball
and a quick show of glittering teeth
in the full glare of camera clicks
with flashes of lightning robbed of their rumble

Meanwhile, outside the world rumbles
and babels
with loud placards of *Make-Poverty-History*
hastily hoisted on talkative tv stations
like Foxed News, all-dat-jazz-era & See-nene!

Seven great men
on the dead man's chest
Ho! Ho! Ho!
they'll cure him of his cough!

The seven great men
(there are the *we-men* too!)
with a taste of flesh stuck to their palates
gather to spend the taste of their rest
on the seventh day

after the creation of chaos
in a world without will
on the seventh day!
After their forebears, full of foreboding
adorned in helmets of heist
sticks stuck to their armpits
denied the uncivilized their dawn
decreed dusk
decreed division, killed cohesion
divinated disease
and death in droves
over captive lands & minds

Seven great men
on the dead man's chest
Ho! Ho! Ho!
they'll cure him of his cough!

What beast beat it into our brains
that seven men
tall
thin
and tawny *we-men*
will impregnate more than a billion others
whose ancestors weren't smart enough
to rob others of their rare resources?

What oracle may have foretold
in thrilling tales of cowry shells
that seven men in Tootal ties
pitched in a cacophony of vengeful voices
in their tribal tongues of a rainbow hue
would agree to thatch our hurtful huts
hew the wood in our backyards

hoe the weeds in our famished farms
draw the water from our clan well
mow & manure the lawn
fend off wars willed by African rulers
along the borders to keep the people busy
Seven men!

Seven great men
On the dead man's chest
Ho! Ho! Ho!
they'll cure him of his cough!

Then there's their rhetoric of pyrotechnics
at which they'd jaw-jaw on wars & conflicts
(with a slid-eye on who's benefited most)
and of undying fires
lit by their audacious foreparents
and stoked by their children
through installed stooges
Soon they simply take on the
African clan heads, their extended tools
who lie thick on their tainted thrones
puffy like the *puff-puff* of my school days
like some rustic czars of Russian reign
engaged in comic rituals of stagecraft
which they gabble like geese as statecraft

Seven great men
on the dead man's chest
Ho! Ho! Ho!
they'll cure him of his cough!

Daily we cry for debt forgiveness
and debt relief

amidst ceaseless debt & death creation
And I ask: Which dwarf of a Doe
in our domain today
can ever forgive his political foil or foe?
Which elephant, tetrarch of our jungle
ever forgives an urchin-fling
from a catapulting sling?

Seven great men
on the dead man's chest
Ho! Ho! Ho!
they'll cure him of his cough!

If the gods pawn poverty & plant plenty
which heels will march to their shrines again?
If the gods douse disease & halt ill-health
shall we again cry with supplicating eyes
                              to the clouds above?
If the gods banish famine & fill our barns with grains
which man, which maid
shall again kneel down to pray in awe?

MOGADISHU

Mogadishu
a city of yellow garlands, of bile & tar
a city besieged by trigger-happy killers
where muggers are bigger than the issue
and mujahidins their enclaves of mud huts

Mogadishu
a city of a thousand clamors
a city whose music is *kwapu-kwapu*[*]
where murder now pleads for order
where pirates lipping conches pose as presidents

Mogadishu
Such a broccadacio!
a city of unprepared deaths
a city filled with sluts in queues
coarsed to comfort callous killers

Mogadishu
a city of doom, the vulture's boom
a city which teaches toddlers about gun parts
even as their diapers still wet, await evacuation
where every morning mothers cry before they fry

Mogadishu
a city of opposed mayors
each claiming a clan & a cache of arms
a city where gun-powder serves as dry milk
serves as the icing on the national cake

Mogadishu
a pity of a city
over which principalities
and powers prime their peck
and the poor, vagrant, endlessly rue their fate
a city where homes are borne on human heads
and people, afraid will not cast a glare behind
nor wait to claim back their God-forsaken land

*kwapu-kwapu: Igbo onomatopoeic imitation of the sounds of small arms.

VICTIMS OF DWARF AND TALL WARS

DRUMS WILL NO LONGER LAMENT

(For Chris, poet who died in war)

I never
met you at the dark waters of the beginning
it's now at noon-time when metaphors
                              trip my gait
when the rainbow arched
like a boa itching to strike
that tall teachers teach me
your lean myth in thin lines

I never
shook hands with you that early
                    at the confluence of planes
it's now, June, after Jadum had met his doom
and Armageddon had reaped from this boom
that I smell the strong ink of your Quink

I remember
a sunbird & an eagle, voices hoarse in swan songs
each furrowed in grey, fluffed their scanty feathers
each clothed in black, sat on your youngling shoulders
sun labels glowered on the delta of your armed arms
your hands filled to capacity with a cold barrel of lead
as *ogbunigwe** beckoned you to the feast of seven souls
Chris, then a member of Christ's age-group, an age
when a cane thrown into the synagogue
                              instigates a stampede
A lute on his lip like a lonely shepherd, Chris buried
a youthful creative self in a self-made grave
for which Mazrui rued as in argument with the dumb
and found the dead poet guilty!

See what death does in an abandoned homestead
where no calls are received & none goes out
When the road is lonely, *nduri* the swashbuckling bird
has the right of way, dancing this way & that way,
occasionally nodding its head in self-justification
picking seeds and weeds on the road in heedlessness
See again what death does in an empty sarcophagus!

Chris, whatever they say
and to whom they ever say it
You are the Spanish Lorca of our time
You who matched words
with the act in action
and embraced the 'tion' in liberation

Alas, the wordsmith, like long-fingered winds
                              is no longer warm
Alas, the song-thrush on the bombax tree
                        dumb & wet grows cold
   No more the Egyptian wonders of a pyramidal past
   No more preaching on the gambit of Mother *Idoto*
   The long drums & cannons will no longer lament
   The scorched path of thunder can now be re-grassed
   Gods swollen from a swim can roam around again

Chris, as you took your leave
did you leave us another,
the one to lead us out of these Labyrinths?

Ogbunigwe, a home-made landmine used by the Biafran forces during the
Nigerian Civil War.

THREE POEMS FOR EZENWA-OHAETO
(1958–2005)

OLD B.B

Whoever cares to remember Hatos
must first remember his old blue Beetle
slow—
and deliberately so—
like an adagio
slouchy
stingy with speed
smooth, serene
Which purred like a pussy
through the ways
and byways of Awka
and like a true pathfinder
Old BB was Hatos' motorized muse
Oftentimes in crawling
jerky jolts, clitter-clatter
on the cobblestones of Awka streets
From dear old *tempsite**
the old blue Beetle
lounged forward, pitter-patter
pitapat, pat-pat, rattatto
into dear new *permsite**
on a daily routine of duty
like a man crossing
the shadow-line
of life into death
and vice-versa
At this ritual of life

man & motor forged a union
as each mused to the other
toing
and
froing
on the squiggling construct
of the potholed roads of a suburbia
In the old blue Beetle
the Pathfinder of the muses
Hatos fiddled with his files of invented lines
yet to be fully processed in his kiln of rhymes
In the creepy jerky jolts of his jalopy
on the bumps of Awka roads
the lines formed themselves
into myths and metonymies
the lines lent themselves
into tropes & topoi
It was in old BB
that the many awards were won!
Whoever cares to remember Hatos
must first remember his old blue Beetle.

*Tempsite and Permsite were the short terms for the 'Temporary Site' and 'Permanent Site' respectively of Ezenwa's College in Awka (Nigeria) where he taught many generations of students before he passed on in 2005.

THANATOS

If humans had given thanatos
its due doff of hat
as one should an episkopos
perhaps our land, this land
would've been a Pactolus
or said in lisping lips

a luscious land laundered in lotos
while we, we all
would've been frolicking in fun
But this has not been so
Instead in my land
thanatos is a mugabi
a musaveni
or an nkurunziza
busy as bush rats
boring holes
into their countries' constitutions
demanding every few years
for yet another term in office

In Greek, thanatos is death, is dead
In Africa, death still pulsates with life
This is because here nobody dies
without the thrust
of an enemy's accursed finger
just as indeed nobody really gets to die
And so even my ancestors
of a century ago still live!
No doubt in death, our death
the flesh will fandango in the sandy field
our spirit will splutter in the airy space
our essence a tango in the Elysian plain
Yet here nobody really gets to die
Yes, not when a man
leaves behind him
breathcrafts
and tonguecrafts
Nay handicrafts
and loincrafts
as Hatos did

Hatos, thanatos has done you nothing!
After all we shall continue to sing
your *songs of a traveller*
and like the Okonkwos of Umuofia
we shall shoot your *bullets for buntings*
You once told us, *I wan bi President*
But one president you knew sought a third term,
another with a tooth-gap is returning at all costs
yet the other has already tried three times
It seems past presidents usually forget
something in office!
Please, convince them to let go
or else address them in the ethereal
voice of the night masquerade
or perhaps sweeten our pleas to them
in the enchanting *chants of a minstrel*

No, however we look at it, Hatos
Thanatos has done you nothing.

THE WORRISOME CRIES OF RIVER-BIRDS

I took a walk to the banks of *Orashi**
my water-bottle slung over my shoulder
In such a serene setting
only tiny birds, gnats & dragon flies
held my sway
Some fragrance of wild flowers hung in the air
And so the sexy smell of the jostling
river thistles
Nearby, shrub-stalks danced *awilo***
in the wind
and worms lowered their heads for fear of fish

Then the tiny, twittering birds
the size only bigger than a leafhopper dangled
their faint frames
on equally flimsy floral stalks
their Morris-Minor faces
engaged my uneasy eyes
as if they held me suspect
Soon, as if responding to a referee's whistle
I heard them all in tow twitter *tii****
I unslung my bottle for a tiny cup of thirst
As I raised the tot to my teeth
the river-birds in one taunt twittered *tii*.
Ugbunkwa!****

My water-bottle
tii!
My tiny cup
tii!
My clean water
tii!
to be thrown into a tosh?
tii!

Ugbunkwa!

The worrisome cries of the river-birds
remind me of the ungodly gods
who daily ask us to cast in
even our most precious possessions
including the beloved & the believed.
And I ask:
Are gods always playing
gastronomic games?
How does human flesh taste

in their spooky mouths?
Like ham or hamburger?
What game has no up-and-running umpire?
What game has no settled full-time?
What game favors the same team
on every tournament tangle?
Again, *tii* hung in the air like a purloined poem

I looked this way, and I stared that way
Fear, I dropped my water-bottle into the *Orashi*
but held firmly to its tiny tot.

Orashi is a river Ezenwa may have fetched water from as a little child.
**Awilo, one of the Camerounian musicians that popularized the flamboy-
ant *macosa* music in the 1990s.
***Tii is Igbo for 'put in' or 'cast in'.
****Ugbunkwa! In parts of Igboland it means 'God forbid!'

LINES TO STONES

(For Mamman Vatsa*)

His pall was in his choosing to be a poet
Rather than expend his time
                    in mess time pepper-soup
he retired to a corner
to fondle with pen-heads
Until brutus fished him out & cried aloud:
'As he was waxing poetic, I slew him.'
Our tabloids seeing nothing wrong in that
took it up from there as in a practiced refrain
chose a choice spot
at the feet of the slayer of slayers
echoed back what they heard, bemused
These men usually welcome Caesar with pomp
cheer pompey when he deserves a jeer
howl with Caesar when he trips
embrace brutus, even if greatly bruised
kiss cassius, even when he kills!

When the shining screen of the tv
offered his face for view
and I beheld a crisscross of cicatrices
on his non-smiling face
I told myself:
Yes a poet's face must be made of similar stuff!

Here I declare
a test for their new slogan in our tabloid
which has never fared well in the face of facts
They staked you
at the left hand side of Human Right
and when you read what they were up to

You reached for a poem in your back pocket
and told them: 'I leave you with smiles.'
How could a non-smiling face leave
anybody with smiles?
and I said to myself:
That's like a cockroach
who 'cos of the 'cock' in the name
and thinking a cock is a kin
seeks a favorable judgment
from a jury of crowing cocks!

Poets must never read their lines to stones
else they raise the ghost of Cinna, the poet
slaughtered for a sin called *Badverses*

I leave you
with a muffled adieu in verse, O Mamman
Today, you're their mammon
Tomorrow, you may be the main man
Or perhaps vice Vatsa

*Mamman Vatsa was a ranking soldier-poet, then Minister of Abuja, exc-
cuted on 6th March, 1986 on allegation of planning to overthrow the mili-
tary government of General Ibrahim Babangida.

RECESSIONAL

BUTTER, NOT BULLET

Butter, not bullet
Let's choose chocolate, not cartridge
Between arms & the man
I'll rather say a farewell to arms
Shelving away my quiver of arrows
better anchored in a bow of hope
for a slow play of lights will do
As fruit falls on the dark garment
covering your black skin
what quickly breaks out is light
cast into a warm wind
If twilight comes,
let it come in letters scribbled in smoke
then I'll be lost in the frock of your dark hour
when dusk descends on a vast view of vines,
for after all the sound of bitter kola is one;
                              its taste is another
And we are here, our lips sticking out
warring on worthless words
putting a stress on how war heals the hero
how a prostitute makes a good house wife
No, hardened by a piano of passion
fun is the finality of your phoneme
I raise my wail like a Satchmo sax
altoing in the warm wind

Let me rather settle for the lights
lifted from the veil covering your twitchy eyes
ignited by a quiver of brambles buried in my soul
from where I distil candy granules,
not gun-powder, you know, not gun-powder
When a cross of impassioned tongues wrestles

as in a knot of expired empires
love tastes like a primrose
pilfered from a moist desire
Yes, like a lone white egret of regret
sailing home in the cold harmattan wind

Butter, not bullet
Let's choose chocolate, not cartridge
Between hug & hate, we shall go for love
Between desire & messiah, we shall go for love
It is chocolate, my dear, chocolate

Their bullet aimed at your breast
will halt at the butt of this butter.

AFRICAN SPRING

African spring
shall spring in May
when fireflies
shall fly at the dusk of day
and the flora & fauna
are fed with the husk of hay
then shrubs
shall shoot up in blazing ray
and wrens in the blissful rain
shall reign & reign
with unfailing fun & unfading fare

African spring
shall spring up at the streams
and spring up at the springs
the dwelling-place of princely pearls
the surfing sight of pellucid pebbles
now & again
the sightly scene of shrimps
and the proud place of prawns
crabs
crayfish
and clams
with zeal
shall dance
the xylophone fling
as in a tasty tango
at a fandango fair
there little fishes swing & swim
and their fingerlings with zest
flick & flicker for food

without so much fear
of sharks

then the kingfisher
usually the fiend of fishes
shall kindred with the slippery eel
and do this
do this
with such an even keel

African spring
shall spring up again
then the cows and calves
shall pasture in peace
and udders
freely yield their milk
then wars
and war-lords
shall take to their heels
and sincere slick of peace
shall spring up
in the minds of inspired men
and women
the muscled fists
of might
and force
shall make way
for healthy
hands & handclasps
then the might of rifles
shall turn to mere trifles
the steely swagger-sticks
shall give way
to the wooden walking-sticks

give way to the warming & the wise
then the militant deaths
shall thin down to a string
and zestful life
shall once more spring up in spring

African spring
shall spring up in synch
with such a sauntering swing
then a man of guts
or a woman of pluck
marching with a spring
may stare
the ogre at our unholy helm
in his vile & foul
face
and boldly
blare at him: 'Now my friend
fair's fair;
your fellows
here are in hell.'
Then little children
a sickly sight to see
dour-faced
tear-suffused
orphaned by fate
shall wear a winsome smile
and give a smirk again
as though their fled fathers
shall soon be home for good
then our fear-and-tear terrain
shall give way
for a free-and-fair domain.

Printed in the United States
By Bookmasters